D1544848

SMALL FURRY ANIMALS

Otter

SMALL FURRY ANIMALS

Otter

Ting Morris

Illustrated by Graham Rosewarne

A⁺
Smart Apple Media

It's very early in the morning, and you watch the mist rising from the slow-moving river. In the dim light, you see a few ripples on the water, but there are no telltale splashes.

Stay very still and keep watching. Can you see something dark and furry moving beneath the water's surface? Who is this early morning swimmer?

Turn the page and take a closer look.

You are lucky—not many people ever get to see a river otter in the wild. Otters move about secretively, both on land and in the water. They live near streams, rivers, and lakes where there are plenty of fish to catch. This hunter is carrying her breakfast to a favorite spot on the riverbank, where she'll wait for her mate to join her.

WHAT ARE MAMMALS?

Otters are mammals. A mammal has hair or fur on its body to help keep it warm. Baby mammals are fed milk from their mother's body. Human beings are mammals, too.

6

Otter

Family tree

Otters are members of the weasel family. They are related to badgers, skunks, and minks, which are all hunters and meat-eaters. Otters are the only family members that can live both on land and in water.

Weasel

Honey badger

Badger

Skunk

Streamlined

Otters have a body that is streamlined for speed in the water. But they move well on land, too. An otter can run faster than a man.

Tale of tails

The river otter's tail is about a third of its body length. The otter uses it for powering through the water and for steering. The tail also comes in handy as a balance when an otter stands on its hind legs.

7

Look, there's the dog otter. He's been out fishing, too. Now he makes whistling sounds as he shoots through the water on his back. Perhaps he's greeting his mate, telling her they're going to have a fishy feast!

Eyes wide open

Otters can see clearly underwater, which comes in handy when hunting fish. They close their eyes only when they are asleep.

WATERPROOF COAT

Otters have a short, tight, waterproof undercoat covered with an outer coat of long, oily guard hairs. When an otter is wet, it looks as if it has spiked up its hair with gel. But that's just the guard hairs—the short fur underneath stays dry.

Closing up

When an otter dives, its small ears and nostrils close automatically. Otters can stay underwater for more than four minutes, but most dives last less than 60 seconds. They can swim 440 yards (400 m) without coming up for air.

Webbed paws

River otters have four webbed feet, which are perfect for swimming and diving. If you've ever swum with flippers, you'll know how much faster they make you. The otter's feet have sharp claws, ideal for gripping slippery fish and climbing muddy riverbanks.

TABLE MANNERS

Otters usually finish up what they catch on the spot, treading water while they eat. The fish's head is bitten off first, and fins are spat out. A large fish may be carried to the riverbank. Otters never leave their food for later, and the only sharers are mothers with their young.

After eating, it's playtime. The courting couple dive in and out of the water, chasing and wrestling each other. One game involves throwing a pebble up in the air and catching it before it reaches the bottom of the river. Now they are playing a game of tag. Before long, the dog catches the female, and she makes a loud chuckling noise.

Rock tools

Sea otters dive down between 65 and 130 feet (20–40 m) to catch a meal. They feed on clams, sea urchins, and mussels. To break open the hard shells, a sea otter picks up a rock and uses it as a tool. It lies on its back, with the rock on its chest, so that it can break open the shell by banging it against the rock.

Mating

Female otters are ready to mate and have babies when they are about two years old. The bitch gives off signals to the male by marking spraint heaps with a special smell. Courting couples also find each other by whistling. Some otter pairs stay, sleep, and eat together for several days.

DROPPINGS

Otter droppings, called spraints, have a musky smell. Musk is a strong-smelling jelly made in glands at the base of an otter's tail. Otters can tell from the smell if the maker is male or female and how old he or she is. Spraints mark an otter's territory and are used as a keep-away sign to intruders.

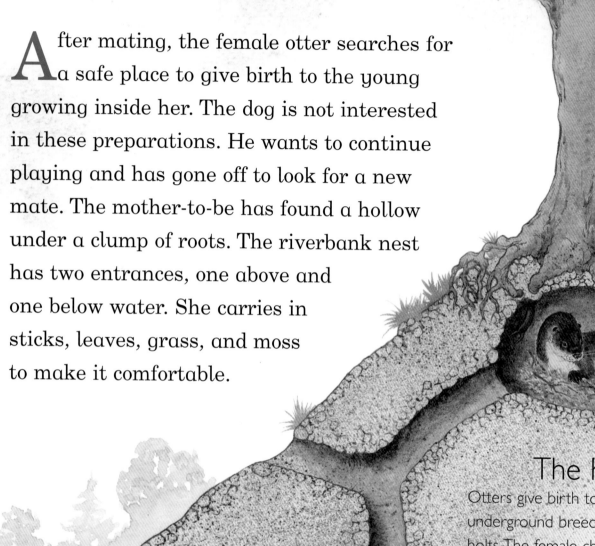

After mating, the female otter searches for a safe place to give birth to the young growing inside her. The dog is not interested in these preparations. He wants to continue playing and has gone off to look for a new mate. The mother-to-be has found a hollow under a clump of roots. The riverbank nest has two entrances, one above and one below water. She carries in sticks, leaves, grass, and moss to make it comfortable.

The holt

Otters give birth to their young in underground breeding dens called holts. The female chooses a well-hidden place close to the river and near a good supply of food. River otters don't dig their own dens, but look for a ready-made tunnel among tree roots, a hole in the river bank, or a hollow tree. She lines the holt to keep it dry.

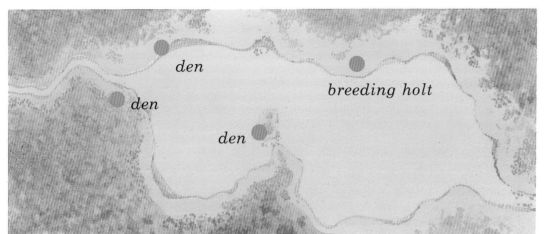

1 mile

1 kilometer

Resting places

After the breeding season, the holts are used by male and female otters to sleep and as places to escape from danger. There are usually a number of dens along a river or by a lake, marked with spraints. Mothers don't leave droppings near their breeding holt, because they don't want other animals to find their young.

A long wait

Eurasian river otters are pregnant for about 62 days. The American river otter's pregnancy can last from 9 to 12 months. This is because the egg stops developing after a few days and starts growing again when the weather is warm and there is lots of food available. The mother gives birth at the beginning of summer.

HOUSE SWAP

American river otters often use a muskrat's burrow as their holt, or they move into an empty beaver lodge. Some otters don't mind sharing with a beaver, especially since the beavers do all the building.

13

Two baby otters are cuddling up to their mother. The blind pups peep like little chicks and suckle every hour. They are covered in gray, fluffy fur and have no teeth. They need their mother's rich milk to keep warm and healthy. Sometimes their father passes the holt, but he never comes to help, and the mother chases him away.

BABY NOTES
Number of litters: 1 a year
Litter size: usually 2 babies
Weight at birth: 2 ounces (60 g)
Length: 4 inches (10 cm)
First solid food: after 7 weeks
Weaning: after 2 to 5 months
Eyes open: after 28–35 days
Adult coat: after 2 to 4 months
Starts swimming: after 3 months

Sea otter pups

Sea otter pups are born at sea, with their eyes open and a full set of milk teeth. They have a special coat of fur, which helps them float once their mother has licked it dry. These water babies can't swim until they are about two months old, so until then, they are carried on their mother's chest while she swims on her back. Sea otters have only one pup every two years.

Giant dads

The giant otters of South America are the river otter's largest relatives. They are about twice as big and very noisy. Unlike river otters, the giants stay together as a family, and the father helps raise the young.

Both pups can walk now, but they are still a bit wobbly on their feet. It's fun and games all day long outside the holt, where they tumble and roll about. With their new, sharp little teeth, they can chew solid food, and they are always hungry. The brothers spend a lot of time calling for their mother, who always brings back a fishy treat from her hunting trips.

Rolling about

An otter spends a lot of time rolling around on the grass, but this is not just for fun. Rolling from side to side is part of its daily grooming activity, helping it keep a sleek, waterproof coat. Every otter has special rolling places within its home range.

Hunting at home

The area in which an otter lives is called its home range. Males have bigger home ranges than females. This diagram shows the range that a female shares with her pups. Certain parts of the range are used all the time, such as dens, feeding places, resting places, sprainting points, and runways for sliding into the water and climbing onto land.

KEY

● *holt*
▲ *sprainting point*
● *rolling point*
▩ *resting point*

SCALE

▬▬▬▬▬
1 mile

▬▬▬▬
1 kilometer

Now that the pups are two and a half months old, they have grown waterproof coats. But they still don't want to get wet and like to stay at the water's edge. Their mother has to drag and push them into the river for their first swimming lesson. Otter babies don't feel at home in the water. One pup hangs on to his mother's back, but the other can't keep his head out of the water. Don't worry, the pups won't sink—their mom always rescues them when they are in trouble.

Swimming lessons

River otter pups get their first swimming lessons when they are between two and three months old. At first they are top-heavy and can't keep their head out of the water or their tail in it. But by four months of age, young otters can dive and catch fish by themselves. Some American river otters carry their young on their back before the youngsters can swim.

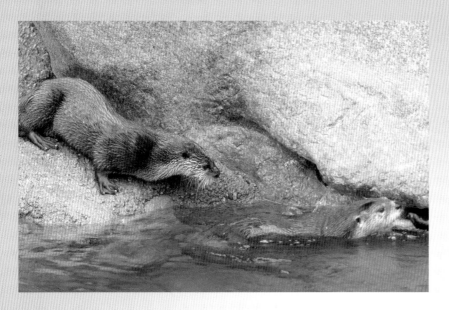

Know your river otter

Different species, or kinds, of river otter have different nose pads. You can tell the otters apart by the shape, size, and hairiness of their nose.

A hairless   B hairy   C hairiest

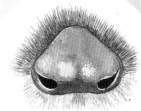

A) American river otter

B) Eurasian otter

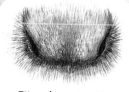

C) giant otter

NATURAL SWIMMERS

An adult otter swims with its tail and hind legs, keeping the forelegs tucked against its body. It kicks its hind legs and moves its tail sideways and up and down.

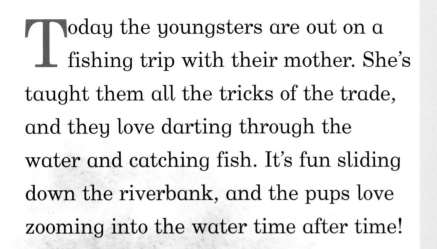

Today the youngsters are out on a fishing trip with their mother. She's taught them all the tricks of the trade, and they love darting through the water and catching fish. It's fun sliding down the riverbank, and the pups love zooming into the water time after time!

A HUNTING LESSON

Wait and watch quietly on the surface. As soon as you see a fish, dive and give chase.

In deep water, dive and grab the fish from below and behind.

In shallow water, slap the water with your tail and drive the prey into a corner or inlet.

Trout and salmon are delicious but usually too fast, so stick to eels and slower fish such as perch.

Dinner time

Otters eat whatever they can catch. Fish is the main food on their menu, but they also catch frogs, insects, worms, and small water birds. On land, they hunt rabbits, voles, and grouse.

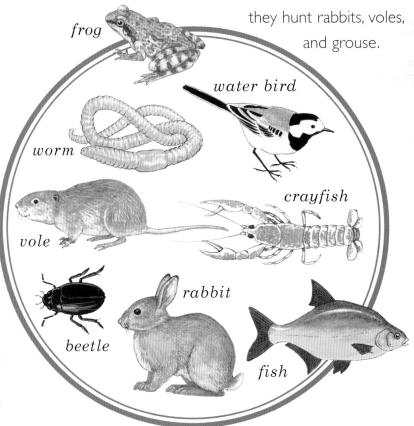

frog

water bird

worm

vole

crayfish

beetle

rabbit

fish

Canned octopus

Some sea otters have learned that discarded drink cans may house a tasty snack. While the cans are drifting out to sea, small octopuses sometimes move in. Sea otters have been spotted collecting the cans and pulling out the canned tenants.

By a whisker

River otters eat about three pounds (1.5 kg) of food each day. In addition to using their eyes, they rely on their whiskers to find a tasty meal. The stiff whiskers pick up the slightest ripple made by a swimming fish.

In the winter, it's not as easy to find food, especially when the river is iced up. So the otter family has to go on long, cross-country journeys, and today they are tracking rabbits. The youngsters can't resist playing around in the snow, and when the mother looks around, she sees that one pup is missing. She calls loudly, but there's no answer. They are far from home, and she knows that young otters are easy prey for larger predators. Then she hears a frightened peep from under the snow. Her silly pup is buried in a snowdrift!

SPEED SKATERS

Otters can reach speeds of up to 18 miles (29 km) per hour on snow and ice. They push off with all four legs, fold them backward, and simply glide. The slides often end with a tumble into a snowdrift.

bald eagle

Enemies

Adult river otters have few enemies in the water. American otters often travel long distances over land and are sometimes caught by surprise. Bald eagles, lynx, coyotes, and wolves hunt otters. In the water, pups are sometimes eaten by big fish such as pike.

lynx

wolf

coyote

Otter chatter

Otters make a number of sounds. Different calls are used for greeting, warning, and questioning. Over long distances, they use a scream that can be heard more than half a mile (1 km) away. Mothers chatter, chuckle, and chirp at their pups, and grunt and growl at strangers and enemies.

FUR TRAPPING

Otters have long been hunted by humans for their soft, furry coats. River and sea otter furs used to be traded, and the giant otter's velvety pelt was especially prized for coats and handbags in the early 1800s. Today, otter hunting is banned in most countries.

23

It's very early in the morning, and mist is rising from the river. Keep very still and watch the two young otters. The brothers are one year old now and can look after themselves. They sometimes see their mother catching fish, but most of the time she is busy with her new babies. In a few months' time, the young otters will leave this part of the river so that each of them can have his own range.

Eurasian coastal otters

Many otters have moved to deserted coasts or even offshore islands, where they find water and food that has not been polluted. The coasts of Scotland and Ireland are good places to find and watch them.

A WORLD OF OTTERS

Otters are found on all continents except Australia and Antarctica.

● African or Cape clawless otter: swamps, rivers, and streams in Senegal, Ethiopia, and South Africa.

● American river otter: throughout North America, from Mexico to Alaska.

● Asian small-clawed otter: throughout Asia; this is the smallest of all otters.

● Eurasian or European river otter: Europe, North Africa, and Asia.

● Giant otter: South America, from Venezuela to Argentina.

● Sea cat: along the Pacific coastline from Peru to the southern tip of South America.

● Sea otter: North Pacific ocean, from California to Alaska.

● Spotted necked otter: African countries south of the Sahara.

POISON

River otters have disappeared from many rivers because their waters have become polluted. Pesticides used by farmers have been washed into the water, poisoning fish and the otters that eat them. In places where these chemicals are no longer used, the otters are coming back.

Females give birth in a den.

OTTER
CIRCLE OF LIFE

In the spring, male and female otters chase each other before mating.

Otters are fully grown when they are about two years old.

When they are seven weeks old,
pups can play outside the den.

Youngsters can swim when they
are three months old, and a
month later they can catch fish.

When they are just over
a year old, young otters
leave their mother's
territory and set up their
own home range.

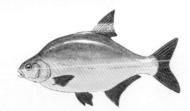

Glossary

bitch A female otter.

breeding den A den where an animal cares for its young as soon as they are born.

den An animal's home or resting place.

dog A male otter.

groom To clean the fur or skin.

guard hairs Long, thick hairs that form part of an animal's outer fur.

holt An otter's den.

home range The area in which an animal lives.

litter A number of baby animals born at one time.

mate When a male and female animal come together to make babies.

28

pelt An animal's coat of fur.

pesticides Chemicals used to kill harmful insects and other pests.

pollute To damage with harmful substances.

pregnant With young developing inside the body.

pup A young otter.

spraint An otter's droppings.

streamlined Having a shape that flows easily through the water or air.

suckle To feed on a mother's milk.

territory The area that an animal defends against animals of the same kind, to keep them away.

INDEX

31

Published by Smart Apple Media
2140 Howard Drive West, North Mankato, Minnesota 56003

Designed by Helen James
Illustrated by Graham Rosewarne

Photographs by Corbis (W. Perry Conway, Roy Corral,
Nicole Duplaix, Robert Holmes, Kennan Ward)

Printed and bound in Thailand

Library of Congress Cataloging-in-Publication Data

Morris, Ting.
Otter / by Ting Morris.
p. cm. — (Small furry animals)
ISBN 1-58340-522-4
1. Otters—Juvenile literature. [1. Otters.] I. Title.

QL737.C25M67 2004
599.769—dc22   2003067253

First Edition

9 8 7 6 5 4 3 2 1